MACHINE LEARNING
WITH
CORE ML 2 AND SWIFT

Karoly Nyisztor

Foreword

Take a deep dive into machine learning with Core ML, and learn how to integrate common machine learning tasks into your apps. "Machine Learning with Core ML 2 and Swift" is a straightforward guide to the hottest topic in the tech industry.

In this book, author Karoly Nyisztor helps to familiarize you with common machine learning tasks. He introduces each concept using simple terms, avoiding confusing jargon. He focuses on the practical application, using hands-on Swift code examples you can use for reference and practice.

Throughout the book, Karoly walks you through several apps to familiarize yourself with Core ML capabilities, including synthetic vision and natural language processing.

Topics include:
- How to take advantage of Core ML
- Setting up a Core ML project in Xcode
- How to use pre-trained models
- Generating predictions
- Using Vision
- Image analysis
- Natural language processing

"Machine Learning with Core ML 2 and Swift" is the perfect book for you if you're interested in machine learning, or if you're looking to switch into an exciting new career track.

Table of Contents

CHAPTER ONE

Introduction

Prerequisites

Before we start our journey, I'd like to show you what you should already know to get started with Core ML and bring your game to the next level by integrating machine learning into your apps.

The first thing is that you should have a Mac with macOS Mojave with Xcode 10 or later installed on it. Mojave is a free upgrade, and you can download Xcode also for free from the Mac App Store.

Although most of the projects you're going to build will run just fine on the Simulator, some demos need an iOS device with a camera.

Since we delve into intermediate topics, you should have a solid understanding of the Swift 3 or Swift 4 programming language.

You should be able to follow along with me if you know what a function is, how to work with closures and delegate methods, how to deal with objects, classes and so on.

You should definitely go ahead if you know how Xcode works, how to create a playground or an iOS project, and how to put together a UI in the storyboard.

And if you're not familiar with these concepts, then you should have a look at some basic books or courses about Swift and iOS programming first.

This book comes with exercise files that you can use to follow along. I suggest you download them to a dedicated folder on your computer.

If you fulfill all these requirements, then have fun with this book.

Terms and Definitions

Let's introduce some of the concepts and terms we use in this book.

- Artificial Intelligence (AI)

Is a term for enabling computers to mimic human intelligence. AI relies on logic, rules and machine learning.

- Machine Learning (ML)

A set of algorithms that can automatically detect patterns in data and then use the patterns to predict future data or make decisions.

- Neural Network

Attempt to model the way the human brain works with layers of nodes linked together.

- Training the Model

Training the model means supplying the neural network with training data, and letting it calculate a formula for combining the input parameters to produce the output(s). Training happens offline, usually on machines with many GPUs.

- Inferencing

Using the trained model by providing it input and letting it calculate the output.

- Framework

A collection of reusable resources and functionality that provide solution to a particular problem area. Users can extend or override the framework but shouldn't modify its code. Frameworks are usually binary packages, so changing their source code is not possible.

- Design Pattern

A reusable solution to recurring design problems in object-oriented systems.

What is Machine Learning?

The term machine learning was introduced in 1959 by Arthur Samuel, an American artificial intelligence pioneer.

He defined machine learning as the "field of study that gives computers the ability to learn without being explicitly programmed."

A computer program is said to learn if it keeps improving its performance on a specific task.

So, what does that actually mean? For example, we could write a program that predicts travel times.

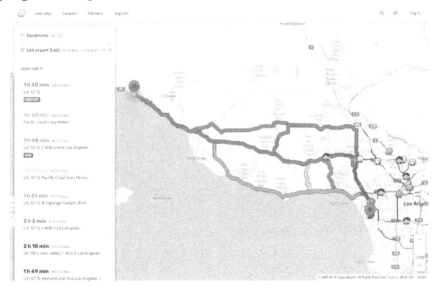

This kind of problem can't be solved by numerical means alone. The program would analyze past and actual traffic data. The more data it analyzes, that is, the more the program learns, the better predictions it makes.

The driving times provided by our program won't be 100% accurate. Better learning algorithms and more statistical data improve the accuracy of these predictions. However, real-world problems are overly complicated, and providing a perfect solution is usually not possible.

For example, the driving times provided by *Waze* - https://www.waze.com - are reasonably accurate. However, you can't expect to arrive precisely at the predicted time. Traffic conditions may have changed by the time you hop in your car. Rest stops, driving speed and other factors will affect your travel time.

Another example is your iPhone camera's facial recognition feature. Sometimes, it fails to detect a face, other times it finds faces where it's not supposed to.

The accuracy of machine learning algorithms can be improved by providing more data. This is how Siri learns to understand what we're saying.

And it works surprisingly well. Besides basic commands like "Call Peter," Siri recognizes complex sentences like "Send a message to Emily on her mobile saying I'll be late" or "Make a reservation at a romantic Italian restaurant tonight at 7 pm."

Programs like Siri keep improving their knowledge by gathering and analyzing as many examples as possible.

Supervised and Unsupervised Machine Learning

Machine learning works in two distinct ways:

☐ Supervised Learning

Requires a preliminary training phase. We provide a set of training data, and the system uses the samples to fine-tune a trained model. This model (also called predictor) can then predict accurate conclusion from new input. To create a good predictor, the training data needs to be diverse, and we must provide the right amount of samples.The following is an example of training samples used to train a flower image classifier:

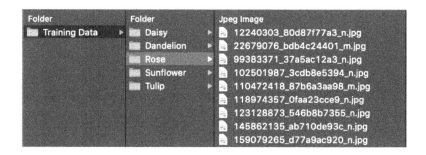

The training data consists of images of flowers grouped by folders labels according to their content. Each folder must include enough images and must contain about the same number of files in each folder.

- **Unsupervised Machine Learning**

This process does not rely on training data. Instead, we feed the system with a considerable amount of data and let it find patterns and correlations therein. For example, we could use unsupervised learning to group a set of websites by topic (science, entertainment, sports, technology, etc.).

To sum it up, supervised learning is about training a predictor using a set of pre-defined, labeled examples and using that predictor to come up with conclusions for new input. In unsupervised learning, the system finds the patterns directly from the input data.

This book discusses supervised learning. We're going to train new models using training examples or use pre-trained data made available by Apple or third parties.

The Machine Learning Model

To use supervised machine learning in an app, we need to:

1. Collect training examples
2. Train a machine learning model / predictor
3. Use the model to come up with conclusions from new input

With pre-trained models, we can skip the first two steps.

A machine learning model can provide predictions for given input. But before it can output those predictions, the model must be trained.

The training is where the learning takes place. When we train our model, we need two things: training examples, that is, sample data. And we also need a system that can learn from the provided training examples.

The system uses the examples to infer rules for producing accurate predictions.

The sample data set needs to be large enough and random. In other words, the training set must be statistically significant. If the data set used for training is too small or not random enough, it will produce inaccurate predictions.

Here's an example to help you understand how the training

actually works.

Spam detection is a classic use of machine learning. Let's say that we want to create a model that predicts if a message is junk.

We need to teach our program what a spam email looks like and what can be considered a safe email.

Our training samples would consist of junk emails that contain external links and email addresses. Now, if we applied only this rule, all messages that have a link in them would be classified as junk. Including that email from our pal with the funny cat video. Or the one from our colleague with links to the company's website. That's not good, we need additional data.

How about adding another condition, like all emails coming from unknown senders that include links are to be considered as junk? This approach may sound better, but it's far from perfect. Not all emails coming from unknown addresses are spam.

There's a better way to detect spam content. When in doubt, instead of guessing, the email program asks you to confirm whether a message is junk or not. If you decide it is junk, the system learns from that experience and becomes smarter. The email app keeps improving. Eventually it filters out the unwanted content correctly, without your intervention.

iOS and Machine Learning

Core ML was first introduced in iOS 11.

Machine learning libraries were available also in earlier versions of the iOS SDK.

The big difference is that Core ML is a high-level framework. It provides an easy to use interface, that lets us integrate machine learning into our apps without having to deal with the complexity of the low-level libraries.

Core ML abstracts the complexity involved in machine learning, but it doesn't compromise on speed, memory footprint or battery usage.

To create apps that include machine learning features, you only need a trained model and the Core ML framework or the frameworks built on top of it.

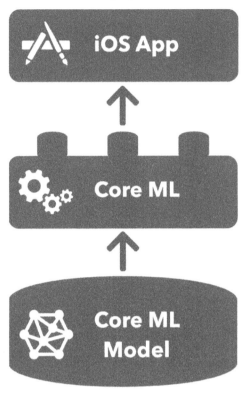

Integrating machine learning into your iOS apps has never been easier. I'm going to prove this by building various projects. But first, let's talk about the high level components we're going to use throughout this book.

Exercise Files

This book comes with exercise files that you can use to follow along. The demo projects are available on Github, and you can download them from the following repository: https://github.com/nyisztor/coreml2-demos.

There are subfolders for each chapter, and in each of these, there is a folder with a start and end project.

If you're jumping in in the middle of the book, you can open up the associated start folder to follow along. If you're working on the book from start to finish, I'll show you when you'll need to open up a fresh project.

If you want to stop and compare your progress to mine, just check in that chapter's "end" folder for the associated project.

CHAPTER TWO

iOS Machine Learning Architecture

A High-Level View

In this chapter, we're going to delve into the various machine learning frameworks that are available for you to integrate machine learning into your apps.

The following diagram shows the various machine learning components and how they relate to each other.

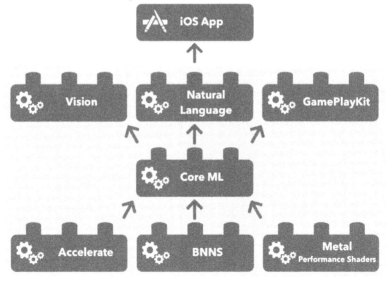

Apple built Core ML on top of low-level frameworks like Accelerate and BNNS, as well as Metal Performance Shaders.

There are also frameworks that rely on the Core ML

framework:

- The Vision framework

Provides high-performance image analysis and computer vision techniques to identify faces, detect features, and classify scenes in images and video.

- The NaturalLanguage framework

Provides natural language processing features, like processing sentences to find out what the user intended to express.

- Gameplay Kit

The game development framework that provides AI to be used in games.

Depending on our needs, we can use Core ML alone or all of these higher level frameworks together. Let's talk about the Core ML framework next.

The Core ML Framework

Core ML is the machine learning software framework provided by Apple. Core ML lets developers use trained machine learning models in iOS, macOS, tvOS and watchOS apps and games.

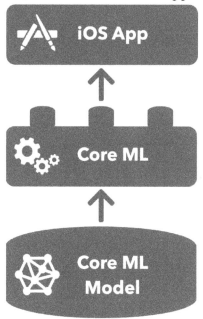

To integrate machine learning into your app, you need to obtain a trained Core ML model first.

One possibility is to train the model ourselves. With Create

ML, we can easily train a model on our computer.

Another option is to download pre-trained models and convert them to Core ML compatible models. We're going to discuss both approaches later in this book.

Integrating the trained model into our app is easy. You simply drag and drop the *.mlmodel into your Xcode project, and Xcode automatically generates the model's interface. We interact with this interface to pass input data to the model and obtain model predictions.

You need to use the Core ML API directly if you want to support advanced use cases, like compiling a model on the device or integrating custom neural network layers into your app.

Natural Language Processing

The NaturalLanguage framework was introduced in June, 2018 at the WWDC. We can use the framework to analyze natural text and perform various task like the following:

- Language Identification

Determines the dominant language of a piece of text.

Detected DE as dominant language for:

"Ich wünsche dir einen guten Morgen!"

- Tokenization

Enumerates the semantic units of a string.

Silence is a source of great strength

Silence
is
a
source
of
great
strength

- Identifying parts of speech

Analyzes natural language texts and classifies parts of speech like nouns, verbs, adjectives, prepositions. The linguistic tagger can be used to recognize names, places and organizations:

Steve Jobs, Steve Wozniak, and Ronald Wayne founded Apple Computer in the garage of Steve Jobs's Los Altos home.

Steve Jobs: PersonalName
Steve Wozniak: PersonalName
and: Conjunction
Ronald Wayne: PersonalName
founded: Verb
Apple Computer: OrganizationName
in: Preposition
the: Determiner
garage: Noun
of: Preposition
Steve Jobs: PersonalName
's: Particle
Los Altos: PlaceName
home: Noun

The NaturalLanguage framework simplifies the challenging tasks of analyzing natural text. We only need to use a couple of types (NLTokenizer, NLTagger) to build powerful text recognition features into our apps.

Besides, we can use the NLModel class along with Create ML to train sophisticated natural language models on our computer using Xcode.

We're going to explore the capabilities of the NaturalLanguage framework by building several demos. So, let's dig in!

The Vision Framework

The Vision framework performs object detection in images. It can recognize and demarcate faces, text and barcodes within still images. Vision provides further advanced features like image analysis on a series of images or tracking objects in videos and camera feeds.

- Rectangle Detection

Finds rectangular regions in an image. You can configure the request to detect only rectangles that conform to certain criteria, like the range of aspect ratios, sizes, etc.

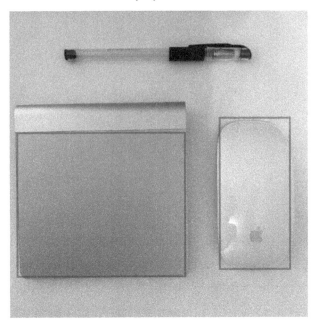

- Face Detection

Finds faces within an image.

- Barcode Detection

Finds and recognizes barcodes in images. The API lets us inspect the content of the detected barcodes. Barcode detection is optimized for finding one barcode per image.

- Text Detection

Finds and recognizes regions of text in images. We can even locate individual characters.

- Horizon Detection

Detects the horizon angle in an image

- Image Alignment

Determines the warp information needed to align the content of two images

- Machine-Learning Image Analysis

Preprocesses photos and classifies them using a Core ML model

- Coordinate Conversion

Conversions between the image coordinates and the normalized coordinate space

- Object Tracking

Detect and track objects from a video in real time.

We're going to delve into some of these topics in the upcoming chapters.

The GamePlayKit Framework

The GamePlayKit framework provides AI and ML features to be used in games and simulations. Don't confuse it with a game engine, though. GamePlayKit is a library of complex algorithms aimed to solve common problems that fall into one of the following areas:

- Randomization

Generates truly random integers, floating-point values and Boolean values. Although there are many other ways to generate random numbers, but none of the available solutions are so easy to use and reliable at the same time.

- Pathfinding

Allows game units to plan and follow optimal routes while navigating the game world. Our game entities will be able to avoid obstacles and optimize their paths without us having to implement complex algorithms like the Dijkstra's algorithm.

- Planning optimal moves

Lets us build games that are exciting to play even against a computer opponent. GamePlayKit employs a form of AI called "the minmax strategist" to plan and suggest optimal moves in certain types of games.

- Autonomous agents

Allows developers to define goals and behaviors that let game characters move and react to events autonomously. We can define goals like "move to location" or "build a weapons factory". We can combine multiple goals in a behavior to define more complex rules, for example "follow path, attack enemy, retreat if health < 30%." This is an area that's definitely worth exploring if you plan to develop games with a unique gameplay.

- Rule systems

Provide a way to define sets of rules and incorporate fuzzy logic to define complex gameplay logic. We design the rules, set the rule system's states and let the rule system evaluate the rules during gameplay.

Fuzzy logic enables a rule system to treat decisions in a way similar to humans. For example, instead of saying "attack if enemy is 5 meters away", we can define a rule that says "attack if the enemy gets too close." The term "too close" makes sense for us, but a program using conventional logic couldn't "understand" it. Fuzzy logic solves this problem by treating terms like "too close" or "far away" as variables rather than discrete values.

- State Machines

Define the possible states in a game and the rules that trigger the transitions between these states. This may not sound so exciting as pathfinding or autonomous agents, but it's the way to go to simplify the design of your game.

- Entities and Components

An architectural design pattern that optimizes our code for reusability and separation of concerns - the pillars of object-oriented design. Although this topic is not related to machine learning, it is very useful and you should rely it to keep your game design clean and easy to maintain and extend.

CHAPTER THREE

Natural Language Text Analysis

What Are We Going to Build?

The NaturalLanguage framework provides natural text analysis features. You don't have to know about concepts like the Hidden Markov Model, representation learning or deep neural networks to integrate natural language processing capabilities into your apps easily.

Here's a sneak peak at what we're going to build in this chapter:

- Language recognizer
We'll build an NLP app that can detect the language of a text.

- String tokenizer
This playground project shows how to use NLP to dissect a text into semantic units. Tokenization stands at the core of most other features, so this is an important exercise.

- Nouns, verbs, adjectives
We build a playground project to identify the various parts of speech. Also, we'll check how it works with sentences written in foreign languages.

- Who's from where?
This smart little demo can recognize names, places and

organizations in natural text.

Alright, so let's dig in!

Recognizing the Dominant Language of a Text

In this lecture, you are going to create a playground that will recognize the dominant language of a given text.

Open up Xcode, and choose File -> New -> Playground to create a new playground. Select the iOS at the top and choose the Blank template. You could also pick macOS or tvOS since the NaturalLanguage framework is cross platform.

Name the project "NaturalLanguage Demo." Click Next and finish creating the project by saving it to the Desktop - or your location of choice.

The first step is to import the NaturalLanguage framework:

```
import NaturalLanguage
```

Next, create a string constant that represents the text we want to analyze.

```
let string = "Ich wünsche dir einen guten Morgen!"
```

To identify the language of a text, you can use the NLLanguageRecognizer class. The easiest way to find out the dominant language is by using the dominantLanguage(for:) type method:

```
open class func dominantLanguage(for string: String) -> NLLanguage?
```

The method takes the text as input, and returns an optional NLLanguage instance. You need to unwrap the optional before using it.

You can use optional binding to find out whether the returned optional has a value and print it to the console.

```
if let language = NLLanguageRecognizer.dominantLanguage(for: string) {

    print("Detected \(language.rawValue.uppercased()) as dominant language for:
\n\"\(string)\"")

} else {

    print("Could not recognize language for: \(string)")

}
```

Execute the playground. It should print the following to the console:

Detected DE as dominant language for:

"Ich wünsche dir einen guten Morgen!"

DE stands for "Deutsch", that is, German.

You can test the recognizer with various foreign languages, e.g. :

```
let string = "空穴來風，未必無因"
```

Executing the playground prints:

Detected ZH-HANT as dominant language for:

"空穴來風，未必無因"

ZH-HANT stands for Traditional Chinese. You can check https://tools.ietf.org/html/bcp47 for language codes.

You managed to identify the dominant language of a text - that is, *the most likely* language. You can also find out a set of language candidates and their probabilities.

First, you create a NLLanguageRecognizer instance:

```
let languageRecognizer = NLLanguageRecognizer()
```

Next, you call the processString() instance method and pass in the text. The languageHypotheses(withMaximum:) returns a dictionary with language-probability pairs:

```
let languageRecognizer = NLLanguageRecognizer()

languageRecognizer.processString(string)
```

```
let languagesWithProbabilities =
languageRecognizer.languageHypotheses(withMaximum: 3)

for (language, probability) in languagesWithProbabilities {

  print("Detected \(language.rawValue.uppercased()), probability \(probability)")

}
languageRecognizer.reset()
```

You should restore the NLLanguageRecognizer object to its initial state to use it for further text analysis.

Executing the playground produces the following console log:

Detected ZH-HANT, probability 0.996545135974884
Detected JA, probability 0.002828312339261174
Detected ZH-HANS, probability 0.0006165678496472538

Traditional Chinese (ZH-HANT) has the highest probability (99%), then comes Japanese with 0.28% probability, and there's only a 0.06% chance that the text's language Simplified Chinese.

The languageConstraints property lets you constrain the identified languages. For example, you might want to only detect English, Spanish and Simplified Chinese:

```
languageRecognizer.languageConstraints = [.english, .spanish, .simplifiedChinese]
```

NLLanguageRecognizer provides a straightforward interface to detect the language of text snippets with minimal coding.

Enumerating the Words in a Text

In this lecture, you are going to implement a string tokenizer.

Open the "NaturalLanguage Demo" playground you created in the previous lesson. Or you can download the project from the **Exercise Files folder, Chapter 3, 3-3, Begin.**

In Xcode choose File -> New -> Playground Page. Name the project "String Tokenizer".

Import the NaturalLanguage framework:

```
import NaturalLanguage
```

Create a string constant:

```
let text = "Knowledge will give you power, but character respect."
```

To tokenize a string, you need a NLTagger instance. NLTagger is a class that supports different languages. Use it to segment a text into units like words, sentences or paragraphs. It can also identify the lexical class or other properties of the detected units.

Create the NLTagger object and initialize it with a list of tag schemes. These tag schemes specify the type of tags you're interested in. To simply retrieve the tokens from a text, the tag scheme array should have a single element with the tag scheme NLTagScheme.tokenType:

```
let tagger = NLTagger(tagSchemes: [.tokenType])
```

Next, set the tagger's string property to the text you want to analyze:

```
tagger.string = text
```

Use the enumerateTags method to retrieve the tokens from a given range of the string:

```
tagger.enumerateTags(in: text.startIndex..<text.endIndex, unit: NLTokenUnit.word,
scheme: NLTagScheme.tokenType, options: [.omitPunctuation, .omitWhitespace]) {
(tag, range) -> Bool in

    print(text[range])

    return true

}
```

The first parameter is the range to analyze. Since you want to parse the entire string, the range should start at the first index (text.startIndex) and should end before the last index (<text.endIndex). The next argument is the linguistic unit. Use NLTokenUnit.word to enumerate for words.

Use NLTagScheme.tokenType for the tag scheme, and include NLTagger.Options.omitPunctuation and NLTagger.Options.omitWhitespace in the options argument to omit white spaces and punctuation tokens.

The last parameter is a block that's applied to ranges of the string. The block has a tag arguments that provides the linguistic tag and a tokenRange argument, which gives the range of the tag. In this demo, you'll only use the tokenRange argument to retrieve the word at the given position. The block's final argument is a reference to a Boolean value. Return true to continue processing the set. If you return false from within the block, enumerateTags() stops the processing.

Execute the playground and check the console output - it should look like the following:

Knowledge

will

give

you

power

but

character

respect

Now change the text to say, Chinese:

```
let text = "读书须用意，一字值千金"
```

You can look up e.g., Hebrew or Japanese proverbs on the Internet to test NLTagger's tokenizing capabilities.

Identifying Parts of Speech

Tokenizing a string is an important feature in natural text analysis, but NSTagger has further, more exciting features. So, let's explore them!

Open the "NaturalLanguage Demo" playground and create a new playground page. Name it "Parts of Speech"and remove the generated code. Next, copy and paste the code from the "String Tokenizer" playground page you implemented in the previous lesson. Alternatively, you can open the project from **Exercise Files folder, Chapter 3, 3-4, Begin.**

Change the initialization of the NLTagger instance from:

```
let tagger = NLTagger(tagSchemes: [NLTagScheme.tokenType])
```

to

```
let tagger = NLTagger(tagSchemes: [.lexicalClass, .language, .script])
```

The .lexicalClass tag scheme lets you find out whether a tokens is a part of speech, punctuation or whitespace. .language provides the language, and .script supplies the script identifier for a token, e.g., "Latn" (Latin script) or "Hans" (Simplified Chinese).

Insert the following code before returning from the

enumerateTags() method's block:

```
print(tag?.rawValue ?? "unknown")
```

Change the scheme parameter's value to NLTagScheme.lexicalClass. Your code should look like the following snippet:

```
tagger.enumerateTags(in: text.startIndex..<text.endIndex,

        unit: NLTokenUnit.word,

        scheme: NLTagScheme.lexicalClass,

        options: [.omitPunctuation, .omitWhitespace]) { (tag, range) -> Bool in

    print(text[range])

    print(tag?.rawValue ?? "unknown")

    return true

}
```

Run the modified code and check the console log. Here's the output (line breaks removed for brevity):

```
Knowledge Noun will Verb give Verb you Pronoun power Noun but Conjunction
character Noun respect Noun
```

As an exercise, change the enumerateTags() scheme to scheme to NLTagScheme.language and then to NLTagScheme.script. Experiment with texts written in various languages like:

```
let text = "读书须用意，一字值千金"
```

NLTagger enumerates the tags regardless of the text's

language and identifies the language and the script accurately. Use this class to segment natural text and identify parts of speech in your apps.

Identifying People, Places and Organizations

In this lecture, you're going to implement a demo that can identify names, places and organizations in natural text.

Open the "NaturalLanguage Demo" playground and create a new playground page called "Semantic Units." Get rid of the boilerplate code. Copy and paste the code from the "Parts of Speech" playground page you implemented in the previous lesson.

You can also open the project from **Exercise Files folder, Chapter 3, 3-5, Begin.**

Replace the text constant with the following:

```
let text = "Steve Jobs, Steve Wozniak, and Ronald Wayne founded Apple Computer in the garage of Steve Jobs's Los Altos home."
```

Next, update the tagger initializer to use the .nameType tag scheme:

```
let tagger = NLTagger(tagSchemes: [.nameType])
```

Change the enumerateTags() scheme parameter to NLTagScheme.nameType. You should end up with the following:

```
tagger.enumerateTags(in: text.startIndex..<text.endIndex,

        unit: NLTokenUnit.word,

        scheme: NLTagScheme.nameType,

        options: [.omitPunctuation, .omitWhitespace]) { (tag, range) -> Bool in

        print(text[range])

        print(tag?.rawValue ?? "unknown")

        return true
}
```

Execute the playground page. You'll get the following console output:

```
Steve PersonalName Jobs PersonalName Steve PersonalName Wozniak
PersonalName and OtherWord Ronald PersonalName Wayne PersonalName
founded OtherWord Apple OrganizationName Computer OrganizationName in
OtherWord the OtherWord garage OtherWord of OtherWord Steve PersonalName
Jobs PersonalName 's OtherWord Los PlaceName Altos PlaceName home
OtherWord
```

NLTagger detects the personal names, places and organizations within the string.

Exercise

48

Change the **NLTagScheme.nameType** value to **NLTagScheme.nameTypeOrLexicalClass**.

Add the **NLTagger.Options.joinNames** to the list of enumerateTags() options and re-run the demo.

Impressive, right?

Throughout this chapter, we explored the capabilities of the NaturalLanguage framework. Natural language processing relies on complex algorithms, but this complexity remains hidden behind a simple and user-friendly API.

CHAPTER FOUR

Image Analysis with the Vision Framework

What Are We Going to Build?

The Vision framework is specialized for computer vision tasks. Its capabilities include, but are not limited to, face tracking, face detection, text detection, shape detection, and barcode detection in still images.

In this section, we're going to explore these capabilities by building several iOS apps. You'll be amazed by how easy it is to implement a:

- Rectangle Detector
We'll create an app that can detect rectangular areas in images.

- Text Detector
This demo will recognize and demarcate regions of text within images.

- Barcode Recognizer
We're going to build an app that can detect barcodes within images.

- Face Detector
An app that can identify faces in a photo.

Alright, let's dig in!

The Starter App

I've gone ahead and created a simple iOS app that will serve you as a starting point for all the projects in this section. You can open the starter project from the **Exercise Files folder, Chapter 4, 4-2, End.**

The project consists of a storyboard file, the AppDelegate, and a view controller. I added an entry in the Info.plist to provide a reason why we need to use the camera. This is required by Apple since the release of iOS 10.

Now switch to the Main.storyboard in the project navigator. There's a camera button in the bottom-left corner of the View Controller's view. The "Connections Inspector" reveals the referencing outlets and the actions fired by the button.

The takePicture action is sent whenever the user taps the Camera button. So, let's check its implementation by switching to the ViewController.swift file.

The method starts by checking if the device has a camera. If there's no camera, it calls the presentPhotoPicker(sourceType:)

method with the sourceType set to .photoLibrary.

```
@IBAction func takePicture() {

    // Show options for the source picker only if the camera is available.

    guard UIImagePickerController.isSourceTypeAvailable(.camera) else {

        presentPhotoPicker(sourceType: .photoLibrary)

        return

    }
```

If the device has a camera, we instantiate an alert controller, and define two actions:

- *takePhoto* lets the user take a photo, and calls presentPhotoPicker(sourceType:) with the sourceType set to .camera.

- *choosePhoto* lets the user pick a photo from the image library, and calls presentPhotoPicker(sourceType:) with the sourceType set to .photoLibrary.

```
let photoSourcePicker = UIAlertController()

let takePhoto = UIAlertAction(title: "Take Photo", style: .default) { [unowned self] _ in

    self.presentPhotoPicker(sourceType: .camera)

}

let choosePhoto = UIAlertAction(title: "Choose Photo", style: .default) { [unowned self] _ in

    self.presentPhotoPicker(sourceType: .photoLibrary)

}
```

I added the two actions to the alert controller:

photoSourcePicker.addAction(takePhoto)

photoSourcePicker.addAction(choosePhoto)

The third action lets the user dismiss the alert view:

photoSourcePicker.addAction(UIAlertAction(title: "Cancel", style: .cancel, handler: nil))

Finally, we present the alert controller.

present(photoSourcePicker, animated: true)

The presentPhotoPicker(sourceType) method creates an image picker controller, sets its delegate to the view controller and the sourceType to whatever we passed as input argument. The last line of code presents the picker:

```
func presentPhotoPicker(sourceType: UIImagePickerController.SourceType) {
    let picker = UIImagePickerController()
    picker.delegate = self
    picker.sourceType = sourceType
    present(picker, animated: true)
}
```

This helper method presents an image picker with the specified source. Depending on the user's choice, the source is either the device's photo library or the built-in camera.

After the user takes an image or chooses one from the image

library, the imagePickerController(_ :, didFinishPickingMediaWithInfo:) delegate method gets called. This is a UIImagePickerControllerDelegate delegate method, implemented in the ViewController extension.

```
extension ViewController: UIImagePickerControllerDelegate,
UINavigationControllerDelegate {

  func imagePickerController(_ picker: UIImagePickerController,
didFinishPickingMediaWithInfo info: [UIImagePickerController.InfoKey: Any]) {

    let info = convertFromUIImagePickerControllerInfoKeyDictionary(info)

    picker.dismiss(animated: true)

    guard let uiImage = info[UIImagePickerController.InfoKey.originalImage] as?
UIImage else {

        fatalError("Error! Could not retrieve image from image picker")

    }

    imageView.image = uiImage

  }

}
```

The method retrieves the image data from the info dictionary, dismisses the picker view and assigns the image to the imageView's image property. Thus, the image gets displayed in the UI.

If you run the app now, it displays an empty view and lets us tap the camera button. If it runs on a device that has a camera, you can choose between taking a photo or picking one for the photos library. The Simulator will only display the second option since it doesn't have a camera.

Next, you're going to implement image analysis features using the Vision framework. So, let's dig in!

Analyzing Still Images using Vision

Before we start the actual image analysis implementation, let's take a closer look at how the Vision framework works. There are three types we're going to work with:

  - The Request

You need to create a request to let Vision detect something for you.

  - The Handler

Gets called after the request completes and lets you process the result of executing a specific request.

  - The Observations

The result returned by the request.

Karoly Nyisztor

Here's a snippet that detects rectangles in a still image. "rectangleDetectRequest" is the request, its type is VNDetectRectanglesRequest. The handler is the completion handler block that's called asynchronously. The expected result is an array of VNRectangleObservation instances. The request might return no observations if Vision couldn't detect any rectangles in the input image.

```
let rectangleDetectRequest = VNDetectRectanglesRequest(
    completionHandler: { (request, error) in
    if let detectError = error as NSError? {
        print(detectError)
        return
    } else {
        guard let results = request.results as?
[VNRectangleObservation] else {
            return
        }
        // evaluate observations...
    }
})
```

Vision has request classes to detect not only rectangular areas, but also regions of text, barcodes or faces within an image. Each request type has a matching observation, like for example VNRectangleObservation or VNBarcodeObservation.

Now that you know how Vision works, let's build our first demo.

60

Implementing the Image Request Handler

In this demo, you're going to create an app that visualizes detected rectangular areas in still images. Here's how the finished app will look like:

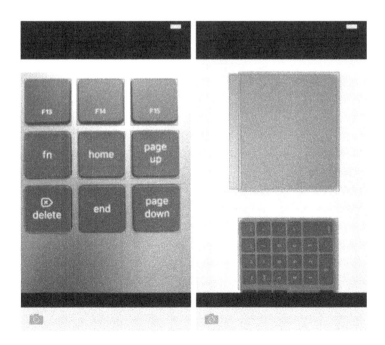

Here are the steps you'll implement in this demo.

1. First, you create an image request handler. The handler's initializer receives the image data and the image orientation.

2. Next, you're going to create a rectangle detection request.

3. Use the image handler to perform the request

4. And finally, implement the request's completion handler. The goal is to visualize the observations, that is, you'll display the bounding boxes of the detected rectangles.

Open up the project from the **Exercise Files folder, Chapter 4, 4-4, Begin**. Now, I show you a technique that's useful to keep your view controllers clean. A View Controller should handle mostly view related logic. Yet, as we keep adding new features, they tend to become bloated. We add some data parsing logic here, networking code there, and our view controller keeps growing. Eventually, the ViewController's code becomes huge and hard to maintain. This phenomenon is also known as the Massive View controller. The easiest way to avoid massive view controllers is through type extensions. We can define a type extension in a separate file and put the logic that should not go into the View Controller there. That's what we're going to do also in this case. We'll create a View Controller extension and implement all the Vision related logic in that extension.

Alright, let's create the extension. Select the Project Navigator, choose "New File…" and create a Swift source file called ViewController+Vision. Next, define the extension:

```
extension ViewController { }
```

Let's not forget to import the UIKit and the Vision frameworks.

The first method is the one that creates the image request handler and performs the Vision request. Call it performVisionRequest(). The method needs the image as input, so declare it like this:

```
func performVisionRequest(image: UIImage) { }
```

Create the image request handler instance next. We'll use the initializer that expects a CGImage instance, the orientation of the image and a dictionary with options:

```
public    init(cgImage    image:    CGImage,    orientation:
CGImagePropertyOrientation, options: [VNImageOption : Any]
= [:])
```

The first parameter is a CGImage reference, that can be obtained from the UIImage. Use the guard statement to make sure this data is available:

```
guard let cgImage = image.cgImage else { return }
```

Now, you can instantiate the request handler:

```
let imageRequestHandler = VNImageRequestHandler(cgImage:
cgImage,
                        orientation: image.cgOrientation,
                        options: [:])
```

For the second argument, you need the image orientation as a CGImagePropertyOrientation type. UIImage has an image orientation property of type Orientation, but the values don't match the ones defined in the CGImagePropertyOrientation enum. Thus, you'll need to convert between the two. The most elegant way is to create a UIImage extension and define a new property that returns the converted value.

So, create a new Swift file, and name it "UIImage+Extension.swift." We're working with types defined in the UIKit framework, so let's import it first.

```
import UIKit
```

Next, define the extension:

```
extension UIImage {}
```

Define a property called cgOrientation of type CGImagePropertyOrientation. It's a calculated property since extensions can't contain stored properties. Now, you simply need to map the UIImage imageOrientation values to their CGImagePropertyOrientation counterpart.

```
extension UIImage {
    var cgOrientation: CGImagePropertyOrientation {
        switch imageOrientation {
        case .up : return .up
        case .upMirrored: return .upMirrored
        case .down: return .down
        case .downMirrored : return .downMirrored
        case .leftMirrored : return .leftMirrored
        case .right : return .right
        case .rightMirrored : return .rightMirrored
        case .left : return .left
```

```
        }
      }
    }
```

Now, go back to the ViewController extension, and complete the request handler initialization by passing in the image cgOrientation. You can use an empty dictionary for the options.

```
  let imageRequestHandler =
VNImageRequestHandler(cgImage: cgImage,
                      orientation: image.cgOrientation,
                      options: [:])
```

All right, you've got an image request handler. Next, you're going to implement the image analysis request.

Detecting Rectangular Areas - The Image Analysis Request

We'll continue from where we left off in the previous lecture, where you created the image request handler. If you've closed the project, open it from the **Exercise Files folder, Chapter 4, 4-5, Begin**.

The image request handler can schedule one or more Vision requests by calling its perform(_:) instance method:

```
open func perform(_ requests: [VNRequest]) throws
```

The method takes an array of *VNRequests* as input. So, let's implement the image analysis request next. Switch to the ViewController+Vision file and declare a property called detectionRequest of type VNDetectRectanglesRequest. This image analysis request can find rectangular regions in an image.

```
var detectionRequest: VNDetectRectanglesRequest {}
```

detectionRequest is a computed property - as you may know, Swift type extensions can't define stored properties. Use the *VNDetectRectanglesRequest* initializer to create a constant called request. The initializer has an optional completion handler that gets invoked when the request completes with the image processing.

```
let request = VNDetectRectanglesRequest( completionHandler: {
(request, error) in
```

If an error occurs, we print it to the console and return:

```
if let detectError = error as NSError? {
    print(detectError)
    return
}
```

On success, the block returns the request. The request's results property contains an array of VNObservation objects specific to the given request. In our case, it would return VNDetectRectanglesRequest results since our request is a VNDetectRectanglesRequest.

Use the VNDetectedObjectObservation if you're not interested in the specific result type. This is a superclass of VNDetectRectanglesRequest and other subclasses, and it provides the information needed to visualize the position and the bounding boxes of the detected image features.

The results property might not contain any observations, so use guard to make sure we've got something to evaluate. Finally, output the observations to the console for debugging purposes. You should remove the print statement from production code.

```
} else {
    guard let observations = request.results as?
[VNDetectedObjectObservation] else {
        return
    }

    print(observations)
```

Now that you have an image analysis request let's finish the implementation of the request handler. Go back to the performVisionRequest(image:) method, and continue from where you left off after creating the VNImageRequestHandler instance.

To schedule Vision requests, you need to call the request handlers perform(_:) instance method and pass in an array of *VNRequests* as input. We only have one request, so create a single-element array:

```
let requests = [detectionRequest]
```

Next, call the handler's perform() method and pass in the requests array as input. The call may throw an error, so call it using try from within a do-catch block. Errors are caught and printed to the console.

```
do {
```

```
    try imageRequestHandler.perform(requests)
  } catch let error as NSError {
    print("Failed to perform image request: \(error)")
    return
  }
```

Image analysis requests are computationally expensive. To avoid locking the user interface, call the perform() method from a background queue. DispatchQueue.global(qos: .userInitiated) returns a system-defined global concurrent queue. The .userInitiated quality of service indicates that we want a very high priority background queue that executes the dispatched tasks quickly:

```
DispatchQueue.global(qos: .userInitiated).async {
    do {
       try imageRequestHandler.perform(requests)
    } catch let error as NSError {
       print("Failed to perform image request: \(error)")
       return
    }
}
```

Now, you have all the pieces, so let's put them together. As a final step, you need to invoke performVisionRequest(image:) after an image is received from the image picker. Select the ViewController.swift file in the Project Navigator. Locate the imagePickerController(_:,didFinishPickingMediaWithInfo) method and insert the following line:

performVisionRequest(image: uiImage)

Your complete image picker delegate method code should be as follows:

```
func imagePickerController(_ picker:
UIImagePickerController, didFinishPickingMediaWithInfo info:
[UIImagePickerController.InfoKey: Any]) {
    picker.dismiss(animated: true)

    guard let uiImage =
info[UIImagePickerController.InfoKey.originalImage] as?
UIImage else {
        fatalError("Error! Could not retrieve image from image
picker.")
    }

    imageView.image = uiImage

    performVisionRequest(image: uiImage)
}
```

Build and run the project. Choose an image that contains rectangular areas like the following one:

If the app detects one or more rectangular areas in the image, the console will display the observations including the normalized coordinates of their bounding rectangle's corners:

[<VNRectangleObservation: 0x2803d3840> 1ABF5ED2-73CC-4945-93F4-92134C5A5D1F, revision 1, 1.000000 [0.341141 0.193694 0.280563 0.208262]]

Next, you're going to display the results in a more user-friendly way.

Converting Coordinates Between Quartz 2D and UIKit

The next step is to visualize the detected observations. Create a new helper method called visualizeObservation(_:):

```
private func visualizeObservations(_ observations:
[VNDetectedObjectObservation]) {}
```

The method takes the observations and draws their bounding rectangles on top of the analyzed image. Since you'll be doing UI-related operations, it is imperative to delegate these calls to the main queue asynchronously:

```
DispatchQueue.main.async {

}
```

Next, check if we've got a valid image. It doesn't make sense to continue if there's no image to analyze.

```
guard let image = imageView.image else {
    print("Failed to retrieve image!")
    return
}
```

You'll need the image's size for the CoreGraphics draw operations:

```
let imageSize = image.size
```

Vision returns the observations in the Quartz 2D coordinate system, that's flipped around the x-axis compared to UIKit's coordinate system. Besides, the results are normalized, so we need to scale the bounding rectangle dimensions to the dimensions of the image.

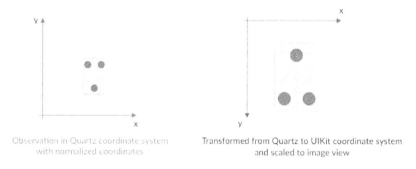

Observation in Quartz coordinate system
with normalized coordinates

Transformed from Quartz to UIKit coordinate system
and scaled to image view

Thus, to render the detected observations, we need to perform a series of transformations on each bounding rectangle.

First, you'll need to flip each bounding rectangle around the x-axis:

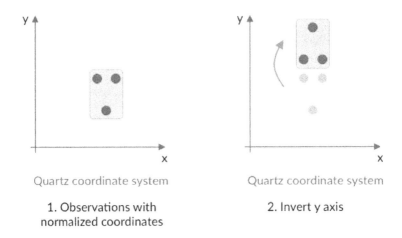

Quartz coordinate system

Quartz coordinate system

1. Observations with
normalized coordinates

2. Invert y axis

Then, you have to adjust the position of the rectangle back by moving it along the y-axis by its height:

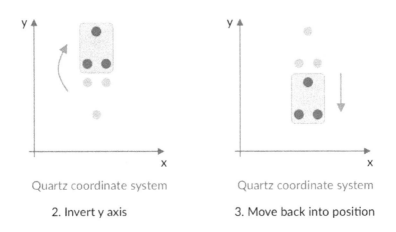

Quartz coordinate system

Quartz coordinate system

2. Invert y axis

3. Move back into position

Let's create the affine matrix that will perform these transformations:

```
// Transform the observation bounding rect from Quartz 2D
coordinate system to UIKit coordinates
// flip vertically and translate back after flipping
var transform = CGAffineTransform.identity.scaledBy(x: 1, y:
```

-1).translatedBy(x: 0, y: -imageSize.height)

You also need to scale the normalized observation coordinates based on the image size.

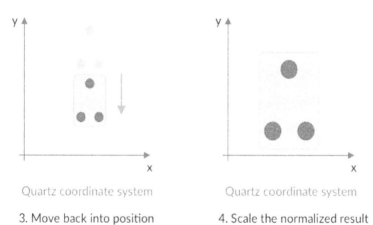

Quartz coordinate system

3. Move back into position

Quartz coordinate system

4. Scale the normalized result

For that, we apply a scale affine transformation:

// Scale the normalized bounding box based on the image dimensions

transform = transform.scaledBy(x: imageSize.width, y: imageSize.height)

After applying these transformations, the observations will be in the UIKit coordinate system and scaled to match the image size.

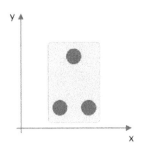

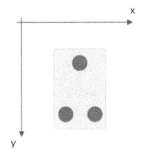

Quartz coordinate system

UIKit coordinate system

4. Scale the normalized result

5. Observation bounding rect
scaled to image dimensions
and converted to UIKit coordinate system

Visualizing the Detected Rectangles

Now that you converted the bounding rectangle coordinates from Quartz 2D to UIKit's coordinate system, you can go ahead and visualize the detected rectangles.

Create a bitmap-based graphics context by passing in the image size. Specify true for the second parameter to indicate that the context is fully opaque:

```
UIGraphicsBeginImageContextWithOptions(imageSize, true, 0.0)
```

Retrieve the context and draw the image in the current graphics context within the boundaries of the provided rectangle:

```
let context = UIGraphicsGetCurrentContext()
image.draw(in: CGRect(origin: .zero, size: imageSize))
```

You're going to draw paths with a custom line, stroke and color properties. Before making these changes, you should save the current graphics state and restore it once you're done with the rendering.

```
context?.saveGState()
// set line properties
context?.setLineWidth(8.0)
context?.setLineJoin(CGLineJoin.round)
context?.setStrokeColor(UIColor.red.cgColor)
context?.setFillColor(red: 1, green: 0, blue: 0, alpha: 0.3)
transparent
```

Apply the transformations on each observation's bounding box and add the rectangular path to the context:

```
observations.forEach({ observation in
    let observationBounds =
observation.boundingBox.applying(transform)
        context?.addRect(observationBounds)
    })
```

Draw the path using the fillStroke drawing mode.
```
context?.drawPath(using: CGPathDrawingMode.fillStroke)
```

We're almost done, so let's restore the graphics state:
```
context?.restoreGState()
```

To render the path, retrieve the image from the bitmap context:
```
let drawnImage =
UIGraphicsGetImageFromCurrentImageContext()
```

Clean   up   the   drawing   environment   by   calling

UIGraphicsEndImageContext(). This removes the bitmap based graphic context we created with the UIGraphicsBeginImageContextWithOptions() call.

```
UIGraphicsEndImageContext()
```

Finally, assign the resulting image to the image view. This will render the path with the detected observation rectangles blended with the original image.

```
self.imageView.image = drawnImage
```

Awesome, you just finished the helper method that visualizes the observations. All we have to do is to use it.

Go back to the *detectionRequest* property and call the visualizeObservations(_:) method. Let's also set some of the request's properties to make it detect only certain rectangles. Your final code should look as follows:

```
var detectionRequest: VNDetectRectanglesRequest {
    let request = VNDetectRectanglesRequest(
completionHandler: { (request, error) in
        if let detectError = error as NSError? {
            print(detectError)
            return
        } else {
            guard let observations = request.results as?
[VNDetectedObjectObservation] else {
                return
```

```
        }

        print(observations)
        self.visualizeObservations(observations)
      }
  })

  // Detect only certain rectangles
  request.maximumObservations = 0
  request.minimumConfidence = 0.5
  request.minimumAspectRatio = 0.4

  return request
}
```

Build and run the app. Tap the camera button to take a photo or select an image. Try to find pictures that feature rectangular areas. The app will highlight the detected rectangles as it did in the following examples:

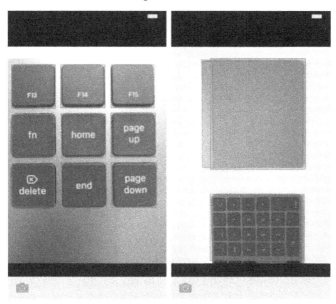

That was quite a lot of typing. However, you've got a stable code base that you're going to reuse in the upcoming demos. You'll only need to make a couple of changes to build demos capable of detecting barcodes, regions of text or faces in still images.

Recognizing Text, Faces and Barcodes in Still Images

In this demo, you're going to update the rectangle detector project so that it finds and demarcates regions of text in still images.

Open the project from the **Exercise Files folder, Chapter 4, 4-8, Begin**.

Select the ViewController+Vision.swift file in the Project Navigator and locate the detectionRequest property.

The detectionRequest property is of type VNDetectRectanglesRequest. Thus, our demo can detect rectangular regions within an image. To detect regions of text, you need to replace the type of the request to VNDetectTextRectanglesRequest:

```
    var detectionRequest: VNDetectRectanglesRequest
VNDetectTextRectanglesRequest {
        let request =
VNDetectRectanglesRequestVNDetectTextRectanglesRequest(
completionHandler: { (request, error) in
        // The rest of the code remains unchanged
```

```
})
```

Set the VNDetectTextRectanglesRequest reportCharacterBoxes property to true if you want Vision to detect the character bounding boxes.

```
request.reportCharacterBoxes = true
```

Now run the app, and use an image that has some text on it. You should see the text regions highlighted like in the following example:

Vision provides further image analysis request types. One of the frequently used features is its capability of detecting faces in images. simulator

Again, you have to change the request type to VNDetectFaceRectanglesRequest:

```
var detectionRequest: VNDetectTextRectanglesRequest
```

VNDetectFaceRectanglesRequest {
        let request = VNDetectTextRectanglesRequest
VNDetectFaceRectanglesRequest(completionHandler: {
(request, error) **in**
                // The rest of the code remains unchanged
        })

And remove the VNDetectTextRectanglesRequest specific code:

        request.reportCharacterBoxes = **true**

The app will now detect and demarcate faces in images:

How about detecting barcodes? Vision lets you do that, too - and
again, you only need to update the type of the request:

        var detectionRequest: ~~VNDetectFaceRectanglesRequest~~

```
VNDetectBarcodesRequest {
    let request = VNDetectFaceRectanglesRequest
VNDetectBarcodesRequest( completionHandler: { (request,
error) in
        // The rest of the code remains unchanged
    })
```

Build and run the project. Choose an image with a barcode. The app will detect and highlight the barcode area like in the following example:

As an exercise, enhance the project so that it detects rectangular areas, faces, barcodes and regions of text at once.

Hint: define all the required image analysis requests as computed properties in the View Controller extension and pass the list of requests to the vision request handler's perform method.

The image analysis features provided by the Vision framework are really powerful, and you can integrate synthetic vision into your apps easily.

CHAPTER FIVE

Training a Flower Classifier on Your Computer using Create ML

What Are We Going to Build?

In this chapter, we're going to train an image classifier model using Create ML, Apple's new framework announced at WWDC 2018.

Core ML allows us to train machine learning models on our computer using Xcode and Swift. All we need is the training data and a couple of lines of code. Building customized models couldn't be easier, as we'll see in the following lectures.

You'll train an image classifier using images of flowers. Then you'll build an iOS app that uses the trained model to identify five types of flowers in images.

Let's get started!

Recognizing Flowers - Preparing the Training Data

We start by collecting the data we want to use for training. The data needs to be organized in a certain structure. We're going to use the directory structure based format, where images are grouped by folders.

There needs to be a top folder called "Training Data" that contain the subfolders labeled according to their content.

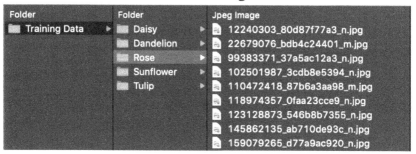

The image files don't have to adhere to any special naming pattern. What matters is the content. For example, if the folder is meant to contain images of roses, then we could name it "Rose," and add at least 10 images of roses. Obviously, the more images we use the better. The images can be of different sizes, but don't use ones that are smaller than 299 x 299 pixels.

You should avoid identical or similar images. To increase the accuracy of the trained model, the image set needs to be be diverse.

Finally, all labeled folders should contain about the same number of images.

We also need a folder called "Testing Data." We put here the images used to evaluate the classifier. There should be no overlap between the images in this folder and the image sets from the training data.

Preparing your data - checklist

☐ Create a "Training Data" folder

    ☐ Create subfolders labeled according to their content

- ☐ Place at least 10 images in these subfolders
- ☐ Use 300 x 300 pixel and higher resolution images.
- ☐ The images should be diverse
- ☐ Balance the number of images for each label/subfolder
☐ Create a "Testing Data" folder
- ☐ Add test images to evaluate the model
- ☐ The test images should not appear in the training data set

Training an Image Classifier in a Playground

You read that right! You're going to train your model in a Swift playground.

Open up Xcode, and create a new playground. It is important to choose the macOS Single View template. Create ML doesn't work on mobile devices.

To train image classifiers, you need to import CreateMLUI.

```
import CreateMLUI
```

Next, create an MLImageClassifierBuilder instance:
```
let builder = MLImageClassifierBuilder()
```

We present the builder in the live view by calling the showInLiveView() instance method:

```
builder.showInLiveView()
```

After running the playground, you should see the following (press ⌥⌘↵ if the Assistant Editor window doesn't show up):

You can now start training the model. The training starts by dragging the "Training Data" folder onto the marked area within the ImageClassifier window.

The training process may take considerable time. The mileage varies depending on the size of the dataset and the performance of your computer.

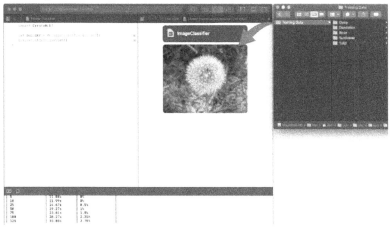

Eventually, the training finishes and the console is filled with statistical data. You can check how many images have been processed, and the time it took to process them. Finally, CreateML tests the classifier with a small subset taken from the training images.

To test the classifier, drag the "Testing Data" folder onto the ImageClassifier window. The folder contains random images of flowers that differ from the ones in the training data set.

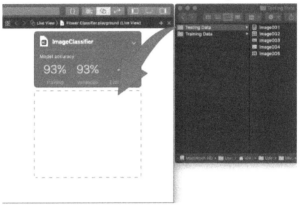

The LiveView shows the predictions:

You can reveal further details by clicking the ^ button. In this example, the classifier recognized the roses with a 99% confidence. No daisies, tulips or dandelions were detected in this image.

The classifier works well, but it wouldn't be very useful if you could use the model exclusively in a playground. Luckily, we can export the model and use it in any app.

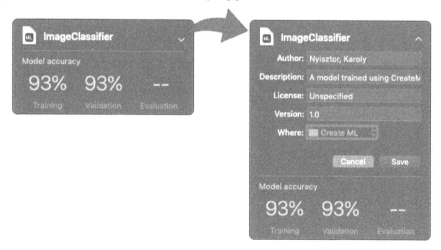

The size of the generated Core ML model is only 66 kB. As an interesting fact, we used almost 240 MB worth of images to train this model.

Next, you're going to use the generated model in an iOS app that can recognize flowers in images taken with the camera or coming from the image library.

Recognizing Flowers - the Starter App

You've created a flower image classifier model, so let's use it in a real app. You're going to create an iOS app that can detect five different flowers in static images. You used images of daisies, dandelions, roses, sunflowers and tulips to train the model. Thus, the app will be able to recognize these types of flowers.

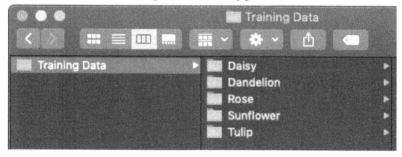

You could enhance the training image set and retrain the model. That would allow the app to recognize additional flowers, like e.g., Jasmine or Viola.

Start by putting together an iOS app. You can download the starter project from the **Exercise Files folder, Chapter 5, 5-2, Begin.**

The app is based on the sample code provided by Apple - Classifying Images with Vision and Core ML. The sample hasn't been updated to Swift 4.2 at the time of writing this book, so I had to fix some warnings.

Remark

If you download the original project from
https://developer.apple.com/documentation/vision/classifying_im
ages_with_vision_and_core_ml, Xcode 10 will perform the
necessary changes for you.

You can save some time if you just use the sample code I provided.

The project consists of a storyboard file, the AppDelegate, a view controller and a machine learning model. The original sample uses the open source MobileNet model to classify images.

You're going to replace this model and you'll also update the relevant code parts to use the flower classifier model we generated previously.

Integrating the Flower Classifier Model

Open up the project from the **Exercise Files folder, Chapter 5, 5-3, Start**. Let's continue by dragging our model into the project navigator:

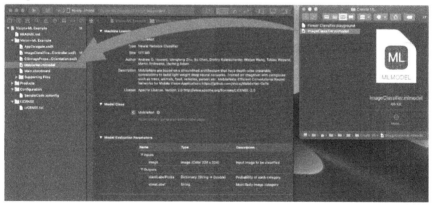

Next, we switch to the ImageClassificationViewController.swift file. The ImageClassificationViewController class contains all the logic that's responsible for loading the model, creating and performing the image classification request and updating the UI with the results of the classification.

The classificationRequest instance property is the image

analysis request that uses a Core ML model to process images.

```
lazy var classificationRequest: VNCoreMLRequest = {
```

Here's where the VNCoreMLModel gets instantiated. Currently, it uses the MobileNet class that was automatically generated for the corresponding model. A VNCoreMLModel instance gets created, which is a container for the Core ML model used with vision requests.

```
lazy var classificationRequest: VNCoreMLRequest = {
    do {
        let model = try VNCoreMLModel(for: MobileNet().model)
```

Let's replace MobileNet with our model's class.

```
        let model = try VNCoreMLModel(for: ImageClassifier().model)
```

The ImageClassifier class was automatically generated by Xcode when we dragged our model onto the Project Navigator.

The next line creates a VNCoreMLRequest instance:

```
let request = VNCoreMLRequest(model: model, completionHandler: {

    //...

})
```

The request takes the model as input, and it runs predictions on that model.

The completion handler is invoked when the request completes. The block has two arguments: the VNRequest that has been completed and an optional error. The request's "results" property contains the results of executing the request.

```
let request = VNCoreMLRequest(model: model, completionHandler: { [weak self] request, error in

    self?.processClassifications(for: request, error: error)

})
```

The block uses a capture list with a weak reference to self, because the view controller might be dismissed before the completion handler is invoked.

The completion handler calls the processClassifications(for:, error:) helper method, that takes the request and the error instance as input arguments. This method evaluates the results and updates the UI and we delve into it soon.

After creating the image analysis request, we set its imageCropAndScaleOption property. This is an optional setting that instructs the Vision algorithm how to scale an input image.

```
request.imageCropAndScaleOption = .centerCrop
```

Finally, we return the request:

```
return request
```

Note that both initializations may fail, hence the calls are made using the "try" keyword, and are embedded in a do-catch block. For example, the VNCoreMLRequest initialization would fail if we tried to use a model that doesn't accept images as input.

If any errors are thrown, the catch block stops the execution by calling fatalError with a message and the error description:

```
} catch {

    fatalError("Failed to load Vision ML model: \(error)")

}
```

Here's the complete code for the classificationRequest property:

```swift
lazy var classificationRequest: VNCoreMLRequest = {
  do {
    let model = try VNCoreMLModel(for: ImageClassifier().model)
    let request = VNCoreMLRequest(model: model, completionHandler: { [weak self] request, error in
      self?.processClassifications(for: request, error: error)
    })
    request.imageCropAndScaleOption = .centerCrop
    return request
  } catch {
    fatalError("Failed to load Vision ML model: \(error)")
  }
}()
```

Displaying Predictions

Let's continue from where we left off in the previous section. Open up the project from the **Exercise Files folder, Chapter 5, 5-4, Start** in case you haven't open it already.

Next, let's take a closer look at the processClassifications(for:, error:) helper method.

First, we need to make sure that the UI-logic is performed on the main UI thread. That's required since the VNCoreMLRequest's completion handler might be called on a background thread.

```
func processClassifications(for request: VNRequest, error: Error?) {

    DispatchQueue.main.async {
```

Remark
I'd recommend delegating UI-calls that occur in completion handlers to the main queue. Blocks get usually invoked in a background queue (unless explicitly stated otherwise), and preforming UI-related tasks from a background queue can have many side-effects.

The request's results property is evaluated next. If its empty, the classificationLabel's text property is assigned the text

"Unable to classify image" and the method returns:

```
func processClassifications(for request: VNRequest, error: Error?) {

DispatchQueue.main.async {

  guard let results = request.results else {

    self.classificationLabel.text = "Unable to classify
image.\n\(error!.localizedDescription)"

    return

  }
```

To understand where this classificationLabel is coming from, we need to take a look the the application's Main.storyboard:

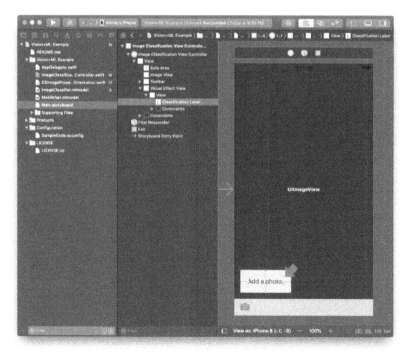

The classification label is embedded in a view that's displayed in the bottom-left part of the application's UI. Here's where all the user-facing messages will be displayed.

Let's continue with the helper method's implementation in the ImageClassificationViewController.swift file. If the request's results property is not empty, we continue by checking its contents.

We are running an image analysis request, and the classification information will be an array of VNClassificationObservation.

```
let classifications = results as! [VNClassificationObservation]
```

If the resulting array is empty, we update the label's text property:

```
if classifications.isEmpty {

    self.classificationLabel.text = "Nothing recognized."

}
```

Otherwise, we create a string with the top classifications ranked by confidence and display it in the UI. The classifications array contains the classifications ranked by confidence. The prefix() array method returns the two highest ranked classifications.

```
} else {

    // Display top classifications ranked by confidence in the UI.

    let topClassifications = classifications.prefix(2)
```

Next, the map(_:) method's closure is called for each item in the topClassifications array.

```
let descriptions = topClassifications.map { classification in

    // Formats the classification for display; e.g. "(0.37) cliff, drop, drop-off".

    return String(format: "  (%.2f) %@", classification.confidence,
classification.identifier)

}
```

This returns an array of maximum two formatted strings in the form:

```
["(0.92) Rose", "(0.04) Tulip"]
```

Finally, we compose a string with the classifications and assign it to the label:

```
        self.classificationLabel.text = "Classification:\n" +
descriptions.joined(separator: "\n")

    }

  }

}
```

Here's the complete method for reference:

```
func processClassifications(for request: VNRequest, error: Error?) {

  DispatchQueue.main.async {

    guard let results = request.results else {

        self.classificationLabel.text = "Unable to classify
image.\n\(error!.localizedDescription)"

        return

    }
```

```
// The `results` will always be `VNClassificationObservation`s, as specified by
the Core ML model in this project.

    let classifications = results as! [VNClassificationObservation]


    if classifications.isEmpty {

        self.classificationLabel.text = "Nothing recognized."

    } else {

        // Display top classifications ranked by confidence in the UI.

        let topClassifications = classifications.prefix(2)

        let descriptions = topClassifications.map { classification in

            // Formats the classification for display; e.g. "(0.37) cliff, drop, drop-off".

            return String(format: "  (%.2f) %@", classification.confidence,
classification.identifier)

        }

        self.classificationLabel.text = "Classification:\n" +
descriptions.joined(separator: "\n")

    }

  }

}
```

Picking an Image

We discussed so far how to integrate the image analysis model in our app, and how to create an image analysis request. Now you have all the pieces required to perform the request.

Let's continue with the project from the **Exercise Files folder, Chapter 5, 5-7, Begin**.

Switch to the Main.storyboard in the project navigator. There's a camera button in the bottom-left corner of the Image Classification View Controller's view. The "Connections Inspector" reveals the referencing outlets and the actions fired by the button.

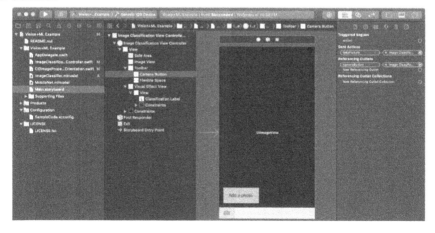

The takePicture action is sent whenever the user taps the

The method starts by checking if the device has a camera. If there's no camera, it calls the presentPhotoPicker(sourceType:) method with the sourceType set to .photoLibrary.

```
@IBAction func takePicture() {

    // Show options for the source picker only if the camera is available.

    guard UIImagePickerController.isSourceTypeAvailable(.camera) else {

        presentPhotoPicker(sourceType: .photoLibrary)

        return

    }
```

If the device has a camera, we instantiate an alert controller, and define two actions:

- *takePhoto* lets the user take a photo, and calls presentPhotoPicker(sourceType:) with the sourceType set to .camera.

- *choosePhoto* lets the user pick a photo from the image library, and calls presentPhotoPicker(sourceType:) with the sourceType set to .photoLibrary.

```
    let photoSourcePicker = UIAlertController()

    let takePhoto = UIAlertAction(title: "Take Photo", style: .default) { [unowned self] _ in

        self.presentPhotoPicker(sourceType: .camera)

    }
```

```
let choosePhoto = UIAlertAction(title: "Choose Photo", style: .default) {
[unowned self] _ in

    self.presentPhotoPicker(sourceType: .photoLibrary)

}
```

We add the two actions to the alert controller:

```
photoSourcePicker.addAction(takePhoto)
```

```
photoSourcePicker.addAction(choosePhoto)
```

And a third action is added that lets the user dismiss the alert view:

```
photoSourcePicker.addAction(UIAlertAction(title: "Cancel", style: .cancel,
handler: nil))
```

Finally, we present the alert controller.

```
present(photoSourcePicker, animated: true)
```

The presentPhotoPicker(sourceType) method creates an image picker controller, sets its delegate to the view controller and the sourceType to whatever we passed as input argument. The last line of code presents the picker:

```
func presentPhotoPicker(sourceType: UIImagePickerController.SourceType) {

let picker = UIImagePickerController()

picker.delegate = self

picker.sourceType = sourceType

present(picker, animated: true)
```

}

This helper method presents an image picker with the specified source. Depending on the user's choice, the source is either the device's photo library or the built-in camera.

Performing the Image Analysis Request

In this lecture, we finish the source code inspection. You can find the project in the **Exercise Files folder, Chapter 5, 5-4, End**.

After the user takes an image or chooses one from the image library, the imagePickerController(_ :, didFinishPickingMediaWithInfo:) delegate method gets called. This is a UIImagePickerControllerDelegate delegate method, implemented in the ImageClassificationViewController extension.

```
extension ImageClassificationViewController: UIImagePickerControllerDelegate,
UINavigationControllerDelegate {

    func imagePickerController(_ picker: UIImagePickerController,
didFinishPickingMediaWithInfo info: [UIImagePickerController.InfoKey: Any]) {

        let info = convertFromUIImagePickerControllerInfoKeyDictionary(info)

        picker.dismiss(animated: true)

        let image =
info[convertFromUIImagePickerControllerInfoKey(UIImagePickerController.InfoK
ey.originalImage)] as! UIImage
```

```
imageView.image = image

updateClassifications(for: image)

  }

}
```

The method retrieves the image data from the info dictionary, dismisses the picker view and assigns the image to the imageView's image property. Thus, the image gets displayed in the UI.

Finally, we call updateClassifications(for:). This is the method that performs the actual image classification request, so let's take a look at it.

It starts by updating the label to show that the process of classifying the images has started:

```
func updateClassifications(for image: UIImage) {

  classificationLabel.text = "Classifying..."
```

Then, we use the CGImagePropertyOrientation extension to convert the image orientation from UIImageOrientation to a corresponding CGImagePropertyOrientation. The image also needs to be converted from UIImage to CIImage, an image representation that compatible with the Core Image filters. We can't continue if this conversion fails, so execution is terminated by calling fatalError().

```
  let orientation = CGImagePropertyOrientation(image.imageOrientation)

  guard let ciImage = CIImage(image: image) else {

    fatalError("Unable to create \(CIImage.self) from \(image).")
```

}

Next, we instantiate a Vision request handler that performs requests on a single image. The initializer takes the CIImage object and the orientation as arguments.

```
let handler = VNImageRequestHandler(ciImage: ciImage, orientation: orientation)
```

Then, the handler's perform() method is called, which schedules Vision requests to be executed. . This method expects an array of image analysis requests as input, so we call it with an array that contains the classification request instance property.

This call might throw, so we need to call it using try and embed it into a do-catch block.

```
do {

  try handler.perform([self.classificationRequest])

} catch {

  print("Failed to perform classification.\n\(error.localizedDescription)")

}
```

Image analysis is a time-consuming task; to avoid blocking the main UI thread, we use a background queue to run the Vision handler setup and execution logic:

```
DispatchQueue.global(qos: .userInitiated).async {

  let handler = VNImageRequestHandler(ciImage: ciImage, orientation: orientation)

  do {

    try handler.perform([self.classificationRequest])

  } catch {

    print("Failed to perform classification.\n\(error.localizedDescription)")

  }

}
```

The classificationRequest's completion handler gets called when the image processing finishes.

As we discussed in Recognizing Flowers - the Starter App , the completion block calls the processClassifications(for:, error:) to display the results.

```
let request = VNCoreMLRequest(model: model, completionHandler: { [weak self]
request, error in

    self?.processClassifications(for: request, error: error)

})
```

Here's a summary of what's happening when the user taps the Camera button:

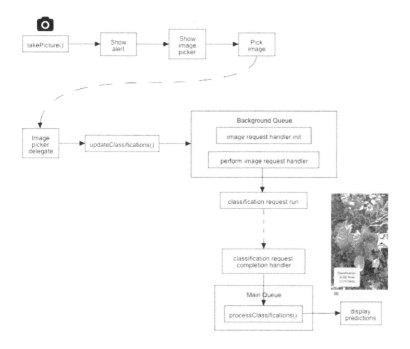

Now that you know the inner workings of the app, let's see how it works.

The Flower Recognizer App in Action

You can run the app either on the Simulator or on a real device. If you choose the simulator, make sure to populate the photo library with images of daisies, dandelions, roses, sunflowers and tulips. As you may recall, our model was trained to recognize these types of flowers.

Make sure to use images that are not included in the training data set. We want to see how well does the model classify images that were not used during the training phase.

Here you can see the results of some of my experiments. The app performed well with images of roses:

But we might get false positives in certain cases:

We could further improve our app by providing a more accurate model. That can be achieved by providing more training data, and we can also tweak the feature extraction settings.

Open up the Flower Classifier playground and run it. Unfold the ImageClassifier settings in the LiveView by clicking the dropdown button:

The "Max Iterations" setting defaults to ten. You could improve the training accuracy by increasing this value slightly. This setting affects the feature extraction execution time, so use it wisely.

You can also use different augmentation operations like noise, rotation, crop etc. to generate more training data from the existing images.

CHAPTER SIX

Determining the Tonality of a Review

What Are We Going to Build?

In this chapter, you're going to train a model that can be used to perform sentiment analysis on a product reviews. The model gets integrated into an app which determines the tonality of a review text. The app tells whether a review is positive or negative.

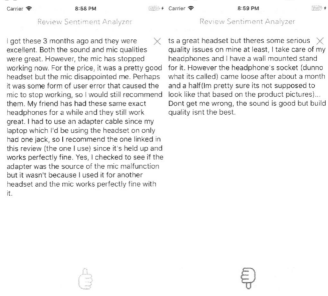

Alright, let's have some fun!

Preparing the Training Data

We can use Create ML to train and test a text classifier machine learning model. The classifier should be trained with a lot of labeled text data.

Create ML can work with training text data coming from a JSON or a CSV file. We can also use the labeled folder based structure we used for the Image Classifier. The latter works well if we have a collection of text files.

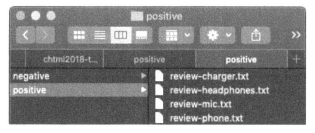

We're going to use the JSON format. The training data consists of real product reviews from Amazon and their corresponding sentiment labels.

Here's a snippet from the JSON file we're going to use:

```
[
  {
    "text": "This is simply the BEST bluetooth headset for sound quality!",
    "label": "positive"
  },
  {
    "text": "After receiving and using the product for just 2 days it broke.",
    "label": "negative"
  },
  {
    "text": "Arrived quickly and much less expensive than others being sold.",
    "label": "positive"
  }
]
```

Our training data consists of about 1,000 Amazon product reviews. Training a natural text classification model requires a fair amount of data. If we provided the full range of possible reviews, our model would provide 100% accurate results all the time.

That's practically impossible, but we should try to come up with a representative set of data. More unique data used for training results in a better accuracy of the trained classifier.

Training a Text Classifier in a Playground

It's time to write some code. Start up Xcode and create a new playground. Choose the "Blank" macOS template. Create ML doesn't work on mobile devices.

First, import the CreateML framework as usual.

```
import CreateML
```

Next, you'll set up two MLDataTable instances:
- *trainingDataTable* holds the contents of the training data set
- *testingDataTable* with the data used to test the trained classifier

You need to provide the URL of the corresponding files to the MLDataTable initializers. So, make sure that the files are available:

```
guard let trainingDataFileURL = Bundle.main.url(forResource: "amazon-reviews",
withExtension: "json"),

let testingDataFileURL = Bundle.main.url(forResource: "testing-reviews",
withExtension: "json") else {

  fatalError("Error! Could not load resource files.")
```

}

We shouldn't continue executing the playground code if these preconditions are not met. Thus, exit by calling fatalError().

Locate the "amazon-reviews.json" and "testing.reviews.json" files in the **Exercise Files folder, Chapter 6, 6-3, Begin/Assets**. Drag them to the Resources folder of our playground.

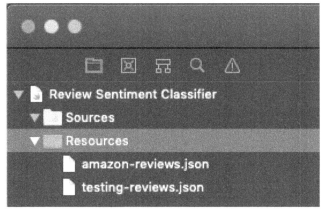

The two files include entries of sentence-sentiment label pairs as shown below:

```
[
  {
    "text": "This is simply the BEST bluetooth headset for sound quality!",
    "label": "positive"
  },
  {
    "text": "After receiving and using the product for just 2 days it broke.",
    "label": "negative"
  },
      ...
]
```

The "amazon-reviews.json" file contains the most entries, since this is our training data. The "testing.reviews.json" file has fewer entries, and we're going to use it for testing.

Create an MLDataTable instance to start the training process. The MLDataTable initializer takes the URL of the training data file and creates a data table with the contents of the training JSON file.

The initialization might fail, so you need to call it using try and embed it in a do-catch block:

```
do {
```

```
let trainingDataTable = try MLDataTable(contentsOf:
trainingDataFileURL)

    //...

} catch {

    print(error.localizedDescription)

}
```

Let's also create a data table for the test data:

```
let testingDataTable = try MLDataTable(contentsOf: testingDataFileURL)
```

Next, print some statistical information about the data tables:

```
let stats = """

==================================================

Entries used for training: \(trainingDataTable.size)

Entries used for testing: \(testingDataTable.size)

"""

print(stats)
```

If you execute the playground, the console log will show the following:

Parsing JSON records from .../amazon-reviews.json

Successfully parsed 981 elements from the JSON file .../amazon-reviews.json

Parsing JSON records from .../testing-reviews.json

Successfully parsed 46 elements from the JSON .../testing-reviews.json

===

Entries used for training: (rows: 981, columns: 2)

Entries used for testing: (rows: 46, columns: 2)

We have almost 1000 entries for training, and about 50 test entries. So, the testing data size is about 5% of the data used for training. This is a healthy ratio between the training and the testing data set.

Creating the
MLTextClassifier

Let's continue by implementing the training part. You can follow along with me by opening the project from the **Exercise Files folder, Chapter 6, 6-4, Begin**.

The training process begins by creating an MLTextClassifier instance. The initializer needs the training data table as input, and we also need to provide the names of the text and label columns. This initializer can throw an error, so we call it using the try keyword:

```
let sentimentClassifier = try MLTextClassifier(trainingData: trainingDataTable,
textColumn: "text", labelColumn: "label")
```

Basically that's all we need to train a text sentiment classifier. Let's build and run the playground. Creating the MLTextClassifier with the provided training data takes only a couple of seconds. We can track the process in the console log:

Parsing JSON records from .../amazon-reviews.json

Successfully parsed 981 elements from the JSON file .../amazon-reviews.json

Parsing JSON records from .../testing-reviews.json

Successfully parsed 46 elements from the JSON .../testing-reviews.json

===

Entries used for training: (rows: 981, columns: 2)

Entries used for testing: (rows: 46, columns: 2)

Automatically generating validation set from 5% of the data.

Tokenizing data and extracting features

50% complete

100% complete

Starting MaxEnt training with 928 samples

Iteration 1 training accuracy 0.496767

Iteration 2 training accuracy 0.919181

Iteration 3 training accuracy 0.959052

Iteration 4 training accuracy 0.997845

Iteration 5 training accuracy 0.998922

Finished MaxEnt training in 0.02 seconds

According to the logs, the text classifier generates a validation set from 5% of the training data. Thus, Xcode uses only 928 samples to train the classifier. The validation set is then used to check the model's performance. You may see different results since the 5% validation data is chosen randomly each time we train the classifier.

The training accuracy is close to 100% after five iterations:

Iteration 5 training accuracy 0.998922

This accuracy is high enough, so the training process stops here. We can retrieve the training and validation accuracy through the classifier's trainingMetrics and validationMetrics properties. Both properties are of type MLClassifierMetrics, which has a classificationError property that represents the fraction of examples incorrectly labeled by this model.

Thus, we can calculate the training and validation accuracy as percentage as follows:

```
let trainingAccuracy = (1.0 -
sentimentClassifier.trainingMetrics.classificationError) * 100

let validationAccuracy = (1.0 -
sentimentClassifier.validationMetrics.classificationError) * 100
```

Let's print these values to the console:

```
let stats = """

-------------------------------------------------

Training accuracy: \(trainingAccuracy)

Validation accuracy: \(validationAccuracy)

"""

print(stats)
```

And here's what this code will print (you may see slightly different values):

```
=========================================
```

Training accuracy: 99.89224137931035

Validation accuracy: 75.47169811320755

These are the results of the automatic evaluation. How about testing the classifier using our test data set? We can do that by testing the model against the testing data table we initialized using:

```
let testingDataTable = try MLDataTable(contentsOf: testingDataFileURL)
```

We need to pass this data table to the classifier's evaluation() method:

```
let evaluationMetrics = sentimentClassifier.evaluation(on: testingDataTable)
```

The evaluation() method returns an MLClassifierMetrics instance. We can inspect its classificationError property to calculate the evaluation accuracy:

```
let evaluationAccuracy = (1.0 - evaluationMetrics.classificationError) * 100
```

We include this information in the console log, too:

```
let message = """

-------------------------------------------------

Training accuracy: \(trainingAccuracy)

Validation accuracy: \(validationAccuracy)

Evaluation accuracy: \(evaluationAccuracy)

"""

print(message)
```

And the log message will now include also the evaluation

accuracy:

==

Training accuracy: 99.89224137931035

Validation accuracy: 75.47169811320755

Evaluation accuracy: 97.82608695652173

Saving the Core ML Model

The evaluation accuracy of our classifier is almost 98%. That means that our model is quite accurate, so it's probably going to provide accurate results with data it's never seen.

To use the classifier in an app, you need to export it as a Core ML model file. You can do that by calling the MLTextClassifier write(to:, metadata:) instance method. This method takes the model file's URL - that is, the path and the file name of the Core ML model file - and a metadata instance that contains additional information about the model.

Set the model file URL to save the file to the desktop - make sure to replace the <user> placeholder with a valid value:

```
let modelFileURL = URL(fileURLWithPath:
"/Users/<user>/Desktop/ReviewClassifier.mlmodel")
```

The metadata instance is of type MLModelMetadata, and it lets you provide the author, a brief description of our model, and a version number:

```
let metadata = MLModelMetadata(author: "Karoly Nyisztor",
    shortDescription: "A model trained to classify product review sentiment",
    version: "1.0")
```

Call the sentimentClassifier's write(to:, metadata:) method:

```
try sentimentClassifier.write(to: modelFileURL, metadata: metadata)
```

And with that, you finished the text classifier playground. It performs two tasks: it trains the model and it saves it to disk.

Execute the playground, and locate the generated ReviewClassifier.mlmodel file on your Desktop. You're going to use it in a moment.

Laying Out the User Interface of the Review Classifier App

You've got a text sentiment classifier, so let's build an app that uses it. You're going to create an iOS app that detects whether a review is positive or negative.

Start Xcode and choose the Single View template. Call the app "Review Sentiment Analyzer" and save it to the Desktop.

Let's start by putting together the app's main UI - here's what you're going to build:

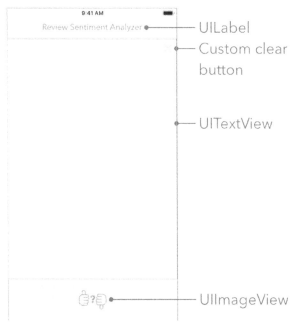

Drag a UILabel and a UITextView and a UIImageView into the main view and set the constraints.

Next, add a UIButton and place it in the upper-right corner of the UITextView. The UITextView doesn't have a clear button, so let's add one - later you'll implement the missing functionality, too.

The following images are available **Exercise Files folder, Chapter 6, 6-6, Begin/Assets**. Drag them into the project's asset catalog:

In the storyboard, assign the image named "clear" as the

button's background image, and set "neutral" as the imageview's image.

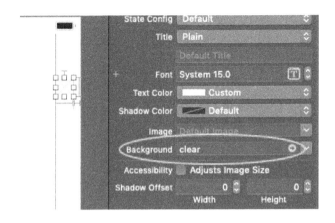

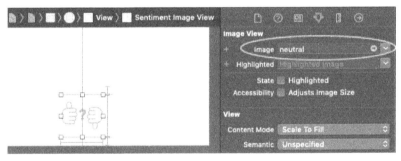

The app will detect the tonality of a review entered or pasted in the text view. To make this work, you should set the textview's delegate first. After selecting the UITextView in the storyboard, drag the delegate outlet from the Connections Inspector to the ViewController. You'll also need a referencing outlet in our view controller's source code. Create it by Control-dragging the textview from the canvas into the source file.

```
@IBOutlet weak var textView: UITextView!
```

Then set a couple of additional outlets:

```
@IBOutlet weak var sentimentImageView: UIImageView!
```

```
@IBOutlet weak var clearButton: UIButton!
```

You're done with the UI part. Up next is the implementation of the text classifier.

Integrating the Review Classifier Model

Let's continue by dragging the model we trained and saved to disk into the app's Project Navigator. Xcode generates a Swift class with the same name for us automatically.

```
class ReviewClassifier {
```

Next, you instantiate a natural language model using the ReviewClassifier model. Create a lazy property of type NLModel:

```
private lazy var sentimentClassifier: NLModel? = {
    let model = try? NLModel(mlModel: ReviewClassifier().model)
    return model
}()
```

The NLModel instance gets created using the NLModel(mlModel:) initializer, by passing in the model property of the ReviewClassifier instance. Call the sentimentClassifier objects's predictedLabel(for:) instance method to predict the sentiment of a review text.

To find out whether the user entered a review in the textfield, you'll need to check if a text is available and the user pressed the Done button. This is performed in the textView(_:, shouldChangeTextIn:, replacementText:) UITextViewDelegate delegate method.

You can keep the ViewController clean by implementing the delegate in an extension:

```
extension ViewController: UITextViewDelegate {

    func textView(_ textView: UITextView, shouldChangeTextIn range: NSRange,
    replacementText text: String) -> Bool {

    }
```

First, check if the textview has some text and the return button was tapped:

```
    if textView.text.isEmpty == false,

        text == "\n" {

            //

        }

    return true

}
```

Then, obtain the prediction by calling the predictedLabel(for:) NLModel instance method:

```
    if let label = sentimentClassifier?.predictedLabel(for: textView.text) {
```

The method might return one of the sentiment labels used in the training data - that is, either "positive" or "negative":

```
[
    {
        "text": "This is simply the BEST bluetooth headset for sound quality!",
        "label": "positive"
    },
    {
        "text": "After receiving and using the product for just 2 days it broke.",
        "label": "negative"
    }
]
```

Use the switch statement to find out the sentiment label, and set the corresponding image to the sentimentImageView:

```swift
switch label {
case "positive":
    sentimentImageView.image = UIImage(named: "positive")
case "negative":
    sentimentImageView.image = UIImage(named: "negative")
default:
    sentimentImageView.image = UIImage(named: "what")
}
```

Finally, let's dismiss the keyboard:

```
textView.resignFirstResponder()
```

Next, we'll add the clear button's functionality. First, define an action for the "Touch Up Inside" event sent by the Clear button:

```
@IBAction func onClearPressed(_ sender: Any) {

    textView.text = ""

    clearButton.isEnabled = false

}
```

If the user taps the "Clear" button, the textview is cleared by setting its text property to an empty string.

The next line disables the clearButton.

The button should be re-enabled when the textview's content changes. You can achieve that by implementing the textViewDidChange(_:) delegate method in out view controller's UITextViewDelegate extension:

```
func textViewDidChange(_ textView: UITextView) {

    clearButton.isEnabled = !textView.text.isEmpty

}
```

Alright, it's time to test the app!

Testing the Review
Classifier App

As you may recall, the training accuracy of the model is close to 100%, and the validation accuracy is above 75%:

Training accuracy: 99.89224137931035

Validation accuracy: 75.47169811320755

But how well does our app perform with real data? Let's check it out! During the upcoming tests, we're going to use reviews that were not included in the training data set.

Here's the first Amazon review - I picked a positive first:

☆☆☆☆☆ **Well worth the price.**
By Jon Veteran on October 6, 2016
Color: Black Windproof

Great umbrella for the price. The ribs appear to we strong and well sewn. The fabric is also strong. Opens and closes automatically (you have to push those compact the length). I'll be ordering another for my wife. It fits in my back and is wide enough when opened that my wide shoulders don't get wet. I usually carry a golf umbrella, so I hope they make those as well.

And the app is right about it:

Great umbrella for the price. The ribs appear to we×
strong and well sewn. The fabric is also strong.
Opens and closes automatically (you have to push
those compact the length). I'll be ordering another
for my wife. It fits in my back and is wide enough
when opened that my wide shoulders don't get wet. I
usually carry a golf umbrella, so I hope they make
those as well.

Same product, but a different opinion:

☆☆☆☆☆ **Super disapointed!**
By Rebekah on January 27, 2018
Color: Yellow   Verified Purchase

Not wind proof at all. The umbrella went inside out the first storm I was walking in! Super disapointed!

And the app thinks this is a negative review.

Now, let's try something different: we'll check some IMDb movie reviews. We trained our model with Amazon reviews, so this is an interesting experiment.

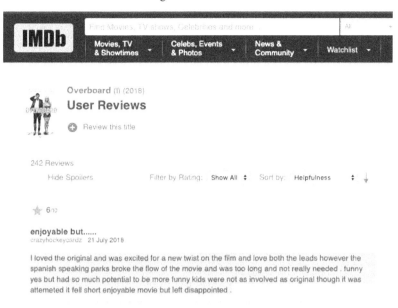

And here's what our app thinks about this review:

And here's another one:

10/10

Don't understand the hate
clsteven 3 May 2018

Seems like all the other commenters haven't actually seen this movie and are just upset that it's a remake. Yes, it's a remake, but it's its own movie, too.

As someone who HAS seen this (and loves the original), I thought it stood on its own, differentiated itself nicely from the original while also updating the story in a way that feels timely and fresh. I also found it surprisingly funny, sweet, heartfelt, and utterly enjoyable. A great change of pace from all the cynical, mean-spirited comedies these days and endless parade of Marvel movies.

181 out of 325 found this helpful. Was this review helpful? Sign in to vote.

Permalink

So far so good, but as you try the app with further reviews, you'll probably notice a higher failure rate than with the Amazon reviews. To improve the accuracy of our model, we should retrain it by adding IMDb reviews, too.

We trained a model that can tell us quite accurately if a product review is positive or not. Instead of looking at each review one by one, we could let such an application process all the reviews for a product, and spit the overall sentiment. It's not unusual that the ratings are not in sync with the reviews.

How about adding more languages? We could train our model to check the tonality of reviews written in French, Korean, German and so on. Machine Learning has opened new horizons, and the possibilities are literally endless.

GoodBye

Congrats, you've reached the end of this book!

You have hopefully found it useful. By now, you've probably become familiar with the fundamental CoreML and machine learning concepts.

Practice makes the master. Try to put the techniques described in this book into practice. Now you have the proof that integrating intelligence into your apps is not complicated at all.

Explore different machine learning models and datasets that are freely available on apple.com, kaggle.com, and similar sites.

I'd love to hear from you! Feel free to email me at carlos@leakka.com. And if you found this book useful, please leave a review or rating.

Useful Links

As an instructor, my goal is to share my 20+ years of software development expertise. I've worked with companies such as Apple, Siemens, SAP, Zen Studios, and many more.

I'm teaching software development related topics, including object-oriented software design, iOS programming, Swift, Objective-C, and UML.

Check out these links for free tutorials, blog posts and other useful stuff:

- Website: http://www.leakka.com
- Youtube: https://www.youtube.com/c/swiftprogrammingtutorials
- Github: https://github.com/nyisztor
- Twitter: https://twitter.com/knyisztor

My books are available on:
- Amazon amazon.com/author/nyisztor and
- iTunes https://itunes.apple.com/us/author/karoly-nyisztor/id1345964804?mt=11.

You can find my programming courses on Udemy, Lynda, LinkedIn Learning, and Pluralsight:

- Udemy: https://www.udemy.com/user/karolynyisztor
- Lynda: https://www.lynda.com/Karoly-Nyisztor/9655357-1.html
- LinkedIn: https://www.linkedin.com/learning/instructors/karoly-nyisztor
- Pluralsight: https://www.pluralsight.com/profile/author/karoly-nyisztor